How S Moon Found Home

by Terry Miller Shannon
Illustrated by Rosalinde Bonnet

Long ago, Sun and Moon
got married.
They went to live in a house
near their friend Sea.

Sun liked to visit Sea. But Sea never came to visit Sun.

"Why don't you visit me and my wife?" asked Sun.

"My people come with me. Your home is too small for all of us," said Sea.

Sun went home and told his wife.
They made their home bigger.

Sea came for a visit.
All her friends came.

More and more water came
into Sun and Moon's house.
The water rose up and up.

"There is no room for us
here!" cried Sun and Moon.
"What will we do?"

Sun and Moon climbed onto the roof.
But the water got higher.
Soon it was up to the roof.

So Sun and Moon rose up
into the sky.
They have lived there happily
ever after.